# Colorful Emotions:

## A Workbook to Help Children Express Their Feelings

### By: Michelle B. Moore, Psy.D.

ISBN-13: 9781505443981
ISBN-10: 1505443989

# DEDICATION

To my mom for her everlasting encouragement and determination

To my husband for his support and love

To my son, Ryan, for being my inspiration

Dear Reader,

The idea for this book began one day when I was working with a student at an elementary school. The student had a difficult family life and had trouble expressing his feelings in a healthy way to understand what was going on inside him. Instead, he acted out in class and caused trouble at home. I began to draw a picture of a person who looked sad, and I asked him how the person felt and why he thought that person felt that way. He began to color the picture, while he talked about a time when he was sad. This pattern continued for several weeks, and the student asked me to draw more pictures each time we met. Over time, *Colorful Emotions*, was created.

It is important for children of all ages to develop a language to express their emotions with others. Sometimes children have a hard time using their words to express how they feel which is how this coloring book can come in handy. This coloring book provides a tool that can help children learn about what their emotions are and how they make them feel. The pages of this workbook will provide children with a useful language to share with the people around them.

The purpose of this book is for parents, teachers, professionals and anyone else who works closely with children to have another avenue to identify emotions. Talk to your children about how to identify each emotion by how your body feels, what happened before you started to feel that way and how you know when someone else is feeling that way. Have the child color the feeling page while you talk. You might even find they talk more when they have an activity to focus them. I hope you have as much fun coloring the pictures in this book as I did in creating each one!

Sincerely,
Michelle B. Moore, Psy.D.
Clinical Psychologist

When I feel *happy*, my face glows, and I smile from ear to ear. I feel like I have wings to fly because I feel so wonderful inside.

What might have happened that made her feel so happy?

What types of things make you feel this happy?

When I feel *sad*, my mouth turns into a frown and teardrops fill my eyes.  Sometimes, I feel down.

What do you think happened that made him feel so sad?

What makes you feel sad sometimes?

When I feel *lonely*, I feel like I am all by myself and want to feel close to someone special.  Sometimes, I feel lonely even when I am around other people.

Why do you think he feels lonely?

When is a time that you have felt lonely?

When I feel *helpful*, I try to help my friends or classmates who are struggling. It makes me feel good inside to help others, and I hope that others would do the same for me if I needed it.

What is happening in the picture that let's you know the girl is being helpful?

When have you been helpful to someone?

When has someone been helpful to you?

HELPFUL

**When I feel *worried*, my mind starts to race with thoughts, sometimes it is hard to breathe and my heart beats really fast.  I also tell others that I am nervous or anxious about something.**

**What do you think happened that has made him feel so worried?**

**When is a time when you have felt worried?**

When I feel *shy*, I want to hide from everyone I see, and I have trouble talking loud enough for other people to hear.

What was it that made her feel so shy all of a sudden?

When is a time when you have felt shy?

When I feel *embarrassed*, sometimes my face turns pink or red, and I wish I could crawl under a rock and hide.  I feel like everyone is staring at me, and I want to run away fast.

What do you think happened that made her feel embarrassed?

What makes you feel embarrassed?

# EMBARRASSED

When I feel *tired*, my body moves slowly, and my eyelids feel heavy.  I start to yawn and am ready to climb into bed and curl up under my covers with my favorite stuffed animal.

What do you think he did today that made him feel tired?

What time of day do you feel the most tired?

When I feel *frustrated*, a big part of me wants to give up and say that I cannot do it.  My body feels tense, it is hard to relax, and I do not want to try anymore.

What do you think made him feel so frustrated?

What makes you feel frustrated?

When I feel *relaxed*, my whole body feels light and carefree.  I am able to let go of any worries or tough feelings and enjoy my day just the way it is.  It is important for everyone to feel relaxed each day to help your mind and body get peace and rest.

What do you do that helps you to feel more relaxed?

RELAXED

When I feel *angry*, my body feels hot, my muscles tighten up, and I feel like I might explode. It is hard to listen to others or to think clearly. The muscles in my face feel so tense that sometimes I even get a headache.

What could have made him feel this angry?

What types of things make you feel angry?

When I feel *silly*, I make funny faces and feel really goofy. Everything makes me laugh. The less it makes sense, the more I laugh, and the sillier I get.

When is a time that you remember being really silly?

When I feel *stressed*, my whole body feels overwhelmed with frustration, and it is hard to think straight. My muscles feel tight, and it is hard to relax.

What could have made him feel this stressed?

What types of things make you feel stressed?

STRESSED

When I feel *proud*, I hold my head high and have a big smile across my face.  It makes me feel good inside when grown-ups tell me that they are proud of something that I have done, too.

What do you think made
her feel proud?

What is something that you
are proud of?

When I feel *disappointed*, there is a frown on my face and sometimes I want to cry.  I feel let down and am not sure when I will feel better.

What do you think happened that made him feel disappointed?

When can you remember a time when you felt disappointed?

# DISAPPOINTED

When I feel *scared*, my teeth start to chatter, my eyes grow wider, and my muscles become tight.  There is something that has frightened me.

What could have happened that made him feel so scared?

What makes you feel scared sometimes?

When I feel *loved*, my heart fills with happiness, and I feel protected by someone special.  I am ready to take on any challenge that comes my way.

Who do you think makes him feel loved?

Who makes you feel loved?

# ABOUT THE AUTHOR

Dr. Michelle Moore is a Clinical Psychologist in New Orleans, LA. She earned her doctorate at Pace University in New York, NY before returning to southeast Louisiana where she was born and raised. Dr. Moore is currently a Clinical Assistant Professor of Psychiatry at Louisiana State University Health Sciences Center where she has the opportunity to work with children and adolescents in communities surrounding the New Orleans area. Dr. Moore also provides psychotherapy and psychological evaluations to children and adults at her private practice in New Orleans.

Made in the USA
San Bernardino, CA
04 October 2016